KERRY WASHINGTON

The Iconic Biography of Hollywood Black Women Trailblazer, (the Author of Thicker than water).

By

ICONIC PRESS

COPYRIGHT ©2023 by:

Iconic Press

CONTENTS

INTRODUCTION

This biography is dedicated to one of the most renowned figures in the American entertainment industry. It is a fascinating documentary that explores the extraordinary life and career of Kerry Washington, one of Hollywood's most accomplished and dynamic actors. This book provides a comprehensive account of Kerry Washington's inspirational path, both on and off the screen, from her modest origins to becoming a household figure.

In this engrossing biography, you will learn the untold stories that led to Washington's rise to fame, which also examines her early years as a child growing up in the Bronx, New York. The difficulties she encountered as a young, female person of color in a largely white field are detailed in the book, along with how she defied expectations to become a real trailblazer. It's fantastic!

It will also walk you through Washington's breakout performance in the highly regarded movie "Save the Last Dance" and her subsequent climb to popularity in films like "Ray" and "The Last King of Scotland." It examines how she can give her characters depth and sincerity, displaying her acting range. From severe dramas to warmhearted comedy, Washington's oeuvre demonstrates her dedication to picking characters that subvert conventional expectations and bring attention to pressing social concerns.

The book does not, however, only concentrate on Washington's acting career. It goes into detail about her activism and charitable endeavors and emphasizes her commitment to advancing inclusivity and diversity in the entertainment business. You will have a better understanding of Washington's drive to use her platform to bring about change via her involvement in movements like Time's Up and her support for women's rights.

It also looks at the effects of Washington's ground-breaking performance as Olivia Pope in the popular TV show "Scandal." It explores how she broke through barriers by being the first African American woman to serve as the showrunner for a primetime network drama in almost four decades. The book explores the show's enormous cultural impact and how viewers all around the world responded to Washington's portrayal of a strong, complicated, and nuanced character.

You will be enthralled by Washington's personal journey, including her adventures as a wife and mother, throughout this renowned biography of the actress. This book explores her relationships, how she manages her personal and professional lives, and the lessons she has picked up along the way.

This biography, which offers a detailed and intimate look at the life of an amazing woman, was written with meticulous research. It honors Kerry Washington's skill, tenacity, and steadfast dedication to changing the world.

Prepare to be inspired and enlightened as you read and turn the pages of this book. Without a doubt, you'll like the ride. Enjoy your time spent reading.

CHAPTER 1

EARLY LIFE AND FOUNDATION

On January 31, 1977, in the Bronx, New York, Kerry Washington was born. Her mother Valerie and her father Earl, a real estate broker, raised her in a close-knit family. When Washington was a little child, her parents were divorced amicably but continued to co-parent her and her younger brother.

Washington was exposed to the diverse and lively culture of the city while growing up in the Bronx. She succeeded academically while attending the exclusive all-girls Spence School in Manhattan. She was involved in community theatre productions and school plays as soon as she realized she loved acting.

She enrolled at George Washington University in Washington, D.C. after finishing high school. She immersed herself in the neighborhood theatre scene while studying sociology and theatre. Washington worked as an intern in the White House for former President Bill Clinton while she was still in college.

Washington pursued additional acting classes as a result of her commitment to her craft. She trained at the Michael Howard Studios in New York City with renowned acting coaches, honing her craft there. Casting directors quickly noticed her talent and tenacity, and she soon found herself starring in theatre performances and making brief television appearances.

Washington debuted in a feature film with 2000's universally praised drama "Our Song." Positive assessments of her performance helped pave the way for her future success. She proceeded to take on difficult and various roles, displaying versatility as an actress.

One of Washington's career-defining moments occurred in 2004 when she co-starred with Julia Stiles in the popular dance movie "Save the Last Dance." She gained widespread attention for her depiction of Chenille Reynolds, a self-assured and charismatic high school student, and it let her access more rewarding possibilities.

With outstanding performances in films like "Ray" (2004), in which she played the wife of artist Ray Charles, and "The Last King of Scotland" (2006), in which she played a doctor caught up in the Ugandan tyrant Idi Amin's rule, Washington's reputation continued to climb. Her reputation as a gifted and adaptable actor was cemented by her capacity to give depth and realism to her characters.

However, Washington faced difficulties along the way to triumph. She encountered structural obstacles and few possibilities for parts that reflected her talent and potential as an African-American woman in Hollywood. She used her platform to promote change and became a vocal supporter of inclusivity and diversity in the entertainment business.

Washington was cast in the part that would launch her to international recognition and solidify her reputation as a trailblazer in 2012. She was chosen to play the crisis management specialist Olivia Pope in the popular television show "Scandal." The Shonda Rhimes-created program made history by featuring a strong African-American woman as the star of a primetime network drama. Washington became a cultural icon as a result of her depiction as Olivia Pope, which struck a chord with viewers everywhere.

Washington has been a social activist and philanthropist in addition to her acting profession. She has fought for equitable representation in the entertainment industry and has spoken out against gender injustice as a supporter of women's rights. She has also participated in campaigns like Time's Up, which works to end sexual harassment and advance equality at work.

In addition to her professional accomplishments, Washington is a devoted wife and mother. In 2013, she wed former NFL star Nnamdi Asomugha, and the two became parents to two kids. Washington has been candid about the difficulties she has had juggling her personal and professional obligations, highlighting the value of self-care and placing family first.

The early experiences Kerry Washington had, together with her brilliance, tenacity, and commitment to making a difference, helped to mold her into the trailblazing woman she is today. Her story serves as motivation for aspiring actors and activists alike, demonstrating that one can overcome challenges and bring about significant change in the world with tenacity and dedication. We'll look into more into these.

THE FOUNDATION

> **Educational Background**

The schooling Kerry Washington had was essential in moulding her into the accomplished and well-respected actress she is today. She went to the Spence School in Manhattan, an all-girls institution renowned for its demanding academic programme.

Washington first became interested in performing while attending Spence.

Washington developed her talents and her gift at Spence by taking part in school plays and local theatre shows. She was able to pursue her artistic interests and hone her acting skills in the school's encouraging environment. Because of her early exposure to the performing arts, she was prepared for a career in Hollywood.

Washington enrolled at George Washington University in Washington, D.C. after finishing high school. She pursued a double major in sociology and theatre, devoting herself to both her academic work and the neighborhood theatre community. She was able to investigate societal concerns and have a deeper grasp of the world around her because to this dual concentration.

Washington also got the exceptional chance to work as a White House intern while she was a student. She gained practical experience in politics and public service while working in the administration of the late President Bill Clinton. She gained a broader perspective and a deeper grasp of the world outside of academia and the entertainment business as a result of this experience.

Washington graduated from George Washington University with a broad base of knowledge and abilities. She was able to hone her acting skills and investigate various acting styles and techniques thanks to her theatre major. Her sociology major, meanwhile, gave her a deeper comprehension of social concerns and the capacity to evaluate the world around her.

Washington continued to seek acting training after receiving his bachelor degree. She trained with renowned acting trainers at the

Michael Howard Studios in New York City, where she attended. Her distinct style and method of acting, which marked her apart from her contemporaries, were able to flourish thanks to this additional training.

Kerry Washington had a solid basis for her acting career because to her academic background, which included her time at the Spence School, studies at George Washington University, and training at the Michael Howard Studios. Her education improved not only her acting skills but also her comprehension of social concerns and outlook on the world. Her success as an actor and her ability to give her characters depth and authenticity can be attributed to her well-rounded education.

> ### Career Beginning

Kerry Washington's college years at George Washington University, where she double majored in theatre and sociology, are the origins of her profession. Washington enthusiastically participated in the neighborhood theatre scene while attending the university, acting in a number of performances and earning useful stage experience.

Washington also had the chance to work as an intern at the White House during her undergraduate years, doing so in former President Bill Clinton's office. Her exposure to the political and public service worlds throughout this experience gave her a distinct viewpoint that would subsequently guide her acting choices and advocacy activities.

Washington continued to hone her acting skills after graduating from college by enrolling at the Michael Howard Studios in New York City. She developed her special style and approach to acting under the direction of renowned acting trainers. She was able to distinguish herself from her contemporaries and get ready for the cutthroat Hollywood industry thanks to this additional instruction.

In the critically praised historical movie "Ray," in which she played Ray Charles' wife Della Bea Robinson, Washington made her breakout performance. She became known as a talented actor to watch after receiving a great deal of praise for her performance. Her ability to give her characters depth and authenticity was underlined in this part in addition to her acting prowess.

Washington went on to star in a number of noteworthy films after finding popularity in "Ray," including "The Last King of Scotland" (2006) and "Django Unchained" (2012). However, it was her portrayal of Olivia Pope in the popular TV show "Scandal" that really propelled her to fame. Washington played a crisis management expert with a complicated personal situation in the show, which debuted in 2012. She received favorable reviews for her depiction of Olivia Pope and received multiple nominations for prizes, including Primetime Emmy and Golden Globe nods.

Washington has continually selected parts throughout her career that go against social standards and highlight significant social issues. She has received accolades for her ability to give her characters dimension and complexity, gracefully and authentically addressing issues like race, gender, and power dynamics.

Washington has established herself as a well-known supporter of social justice and equality in addition to her acting career. She has used her platform to raise awareness of significant topics, such as the dearth of diversity in Hollywood and the value of media representation. She has gained respect and notoriety outside of the entertainment world thanks to her advocacy.

Kerry Washington's early success in her career may be largely ascribed to her commitment to her profession, her broad education, and her capacity to select parts that subvert social standards. Her reputation as a gifted and significant actress in Hollywood has been cemented by her talent, enthusiasm, and dedication to making a difference.

KERRY WASHINGTON BIO

CHAPTER 2

THE RISE TO FAME

T he combination of Kerry Washington's remarkable skill, intelligent role selections, and dedication to leveraging her platform for social purpose has contributed to her climb to renown. From her early studies in theatre and sociology at George Washington University to her breakthrough performance in the highly acclaimed movie "Ray," Washington has constantly shown herself to be a versatile and alluring performer.

Washington's tenure at George Washington University gave her a solid foundation in both sociology and theatre, which enabled her to get a profound insight into societal dynamics and human behavior. This unusual amalgamation of academic specialties surely inspired her acting style and her capacity to give her characters depth and authenticity.

Washington experience at White House intern throughout her undergraduate years, gave her exposure to the political and public service industries. Her worldview was clearly affected by this intimate experience with the inner workings of government, and it gave her a distinctive viewpoint that would subsequently guide her acting choices and advocacy activities.

Washington continued to hone her acting skills after graduating from college by enrolling at the famed Michael Howard Studios in New York City. She was able to hone her abilities and create her own distinctive style and approach to acting thanks to this additional instruction, differentiating herself from her contemporaries in the cutthroat world of Hollywood.

In the 2004 biographical film "Ray," Washington played Della Bea Robinson, Ray Charles' wife, and it was her breakout performance. She was recognized as a talented actress to watch after the film's critical and public reception was overwhelmingly positive. Washington's performance in this part not only demonstrated her acting skills, but also her capacity to give her characters nuance and sincerity.

Washington went on to star in a number of noteworthy films after finding popularity in "Ray," including "The Last King of Scotland" (2006) and "Django Unchained" (2012). But it was her portrayal of Olivia Pope in the popular TV show "Scandal" that really propelled her to fame. The 2012 television series' central character, a crisis management specialist with a complicated personal situation, was played by Kerry Washington. She received favorable reviews for her portrayal of Olivia Pope and received multiple nominations for prizes, including Primetime Emmy and Golden Globe nods.

Her portrayal of Olivia Pope not only demonstrated her prodigious acting skills but also cemented her position as a pioneer in the field. Washington broke down barriers and destroyed preconceptions as one of the few Black women to serve as the showrunner of a primetime drama series, paving the way for more diversity and representation in Hollywood.

Kerry Washington has continually selected parts throughout her career that go against social standards and highlight significant social issues. Washington has utilized her platform to highlight significant social concerns, tackling racism and gender relations in films like "Django Unchained" and delving into power dynamics in her role as Olivia Pope. She has gained appreciation from both her peers and fans for her ability to give her characters richness and complexity.

Washington has developed into a well-known proponent of social justice and equality in addition to her acting career. She has made use of her platform to raise awareness of crucial topics like the lack of diversity in Hollywood and the value of media representation. She has gained popularity outside of the entertainment industry thanks to her activism and dedication to changing the world.

All things considered, Kerry Washington's success may be due to her remarkable talent, clever casting decisions, and dedication to using her platform to promote social change. Her dedication to her craft, combined with her ability to choose roles that challenge societal norms, has solidified her status as a talented and influential actress in Hollywood. Additionally, her activism and advocacy work have further cemented her legacy as a trailblazer and role model for aspiring actors and activists alike.

> ### Wonderful Delivery In "Scandal"

Kerry Washington's breakout performance in the popular TV show "Scandal" cemented her reputation as a household figure and catapulted her to stardom. Olivia Pope, played by Washington, is a crisis management specialist with a complicated personal life. Shonda Rhimes created the show, which debuted in 2012.

For a number of reasons, Washington's portrayal of Olivia Pope was revolutionary. She first broke down boundaries and pushed back against Hollywood's lack of diversity by being one of the few Black women to serve as the showrunner of a primetime drama series. Her selection as the main character in a well-known show sends a strong message about the value of representation and made way for more varied storytelling.

Beyond her ground-breaking casting, Washington gave an outstanding performance as Olivia Pope. Both viewers and critics were enthralled by the depth, complexity, and vulnerability she gave to the role. The character of Olivia Pope was a realistic and complex one since she was a strong, clever, and fiercely independent woman navigating the worlds of politics and power while still having her own weaknesses and insecurities.

Olivia Pope, as portrayed by Washington, was a brilliant example of her tremendous range and dramatic prowess. She shifted between states of strength and vulnerability with ease, expressing a variety of emotions with honesty and depth. Washington's performance had viewers on the edge of their seats and engrossed in Olivia Pope's journey, whether she was delivering potent monologues or displaying subtle facial expressions.

The huge success of "Scandal" can mainly be credited to Washington's magnetic presence and her ability to dominate the screen. The main love story of the show gained complexity from her relationship with her co-stars, especially Tony Goldwyn as President Fitzgerald Grant. The on-screen chemistry between Goldwyn and Washington was palpable, which added to the show's compelling qualities.

Washington's portrayal as Olivia Pope gave her the opportunity to discuss significant social issues and bring light to power dynamics in politics and society in addition to her superb acting. The program addressed issues like deceit, deception, and the blending of personal and professional lives. Washington's portrayal as Olivia Pope served as a commentary on the challenges of wielding authority and the trade-offs involved.

The critical acclaim and popularity of "Scandal" cemented Washington's reputation as a gifted and influential actor. For her performance, she was nominated for multiple awards, including the

Primetime Emmy and Golden Globe. Washington's portrayal of Olivia Pope not only demonstrated her prodigious acting skills but also her capacity to give complex characters life and authenticity.

In addition to her acting profession, Washington's part in "Scandal" had a big effect on the television industry. The programs opened the door for a wider range of stories and greater representation on television. It proved that audiences were ravenous for nuanced, dimensional individuals with a range of experiences and cultures.

Finally, Kerry Washington's breakout performance as Olivia Pope in "Scandal" was a pivotal point in her professional life. Her tremendous talent, along with the innovative nature of her casting, solidified her standing as an industry trailblazer. Washington's portrayal of Olivia Pope highlighted her prodigious acting skills, dealt with significant societal concerns, and paved the way for more diverse television storytelling. Her performance on "Scandal" will go down in television history as a turning point.

➢ Critical Acclaim and Awards

Kerry Washington's extraordinary acting talents, particularly for her role as Olivia Pope in "Scandal," have garnered her significant praise from the critics and countless honors.

Washington received numerous nominations for the role of Olivia Pope, including Primetime Emmy and Golden Globe nods. She received Primetime Emmy nominations for Outstanding Lead Actress in a Drama Series in 2013, 2014, and 2015, demonstrating her constant proficiency in the role. Her powerful and nuanced portrayal of Olivia Pope established her as one of television's leading performers.

Washington was again nominated for Best Actress in a Television Series - Drama at the Golden Globes in 2013, 2014, and 2015. These nominations cemented her reputation as a skilled and influential actor, as the Golden Globes are widely respected in the business.

In addition to these significant nominations, Washington has received various honors for her work in "Scandal." In 2013, 2014, and 2015, she earned the NAACP Image Award for Outstanding Actress in a Drama Series, demonstrating her constant proficiency in the role. Washington's triumphs at the NAACP Image Awards underscore her significance as a trailblazer for diversity and representation in Hollywood.

Washington was also nominated for a Women's Image Network Award for Outstanding Actress in a Drama Series in 2012 and 2013. This award recognizes her outstanding performance as well as the good image of women on cinema.

Aside from these specific honors, critics have complimented Washington's performance as Olivia Pope. Her ability to give the character depth, sincerity, and sensitivity has been constantly praised. Critics praised her for expressing the nuances of Olivia Pope's personal and professional life, as well as displaying a spectrum of emotions with sensitivity and nuance.

Washington's critical praise and award nominations for her performance in "Scandal" show the effect and respect she has garnered for her remarkable acting ability. Her portrayal of Olivia Pope cemented her reputation as an accomplished and important actor in the industry. Washington's accomplishment on "Scandal" not only demonstrated her enormous skill, but it also helped to increasing representation and diversity in television storytelling.

18

➤ Expansion into Film and Production

In addition to her success in television, Kerry Washington has expanded her career into filming and producing, establishing herself as a multidimensional and prominent person in the entertainment world.

Washington's film career began early in her career, with roles in films such as "Save the Last Dance" (2001) and "Ray" (2004) demonstrating her flexibility as an actress. Her performance as Broomhilda von Shaft in Quentin Tarantino's critically praised film "Django Unchained" (2012), however, drew the most notice and appreciation. Her performance in the film, among actors such as Jamie Foxx and Leonardo DiCaprio, demonstrated her talent and breadth as an actress even more.

Following the success of "Django Unchained," Washington went on to play a variety of characters in films such as "The Last King of Scotland" (2006), "The Dead Girl" (2006), and "Night Catches Us" (2010). These roles gave her the opportunity to experiment with diverse genres and characters, demonstrating her ability to adapt to varied storytelling approaches and add depth to her performances.

Washington has moved into producing in addition to her performing career. She was an executive producer on the critically praised HBO film "Confirmation" (2016), in which she played Anita Hill. The film, which focused on Clarence Thomas's contentious Supreme Court nomination hearings, gained international recognition for its dramatic storytelling and Washington's captivating performance.

In addition, Washington established her production firm, Simpson Street, in 2016. She hopes to create diverse and inclusive content that elevates underrepresented voices through Simpson Street. The firm has already produced projects such as the documentary "The Fight" (2020) and the drama series "Little Fires Everywhere" (2020), both of which won critical praise and cemented Washington's reputation as a producer dedicated to creating significant and compelling tales.

Washington's foray into film and production shows her dedication to leveraging her position to encourage diversity and representation in the industry. She has been a forerunner for change and a champion for inclusiveness in Hollywood by taking on varied roles and producing films that prioritize underrepresented voices.

In general, Kerry Washington's move into film and producing has given her the opportunity to demonstrate her talent and variety as an actress while simultaneously campaigning for significant social concerns through her work. Her success in these endeavors cements her position as a diverse and prominent figure in the entertainment business.

CHAPTER 3

K erry Washington is well-known for keeping her personal life discreet. She has kept many facts of her personal life private, preferring to focus on her career and advocacy work. Some details of her personal life, however, have been made public.

As previously stated, she grew up in a middle-class family with a strong sense of community and social justice. Valerie Washington, her mother, was a professor and educational consultant, and her father, Earl Washington, was a real estate broker.

In a secret ceremony, Washington wed former NFL star Nnamdi Asomugha in 2013. Throughout his football career, Asomugha played for the Oakland Raiders, Philadelphia Eagles, and San Francisco 49ers. They are parents to two kids: a son named Caleb Kelechi Asomugha was born in 2016, and a daughter named Isabelle Amarachi Asomugha was born in 2014.

> ## The Asomugha's

Asomugha played in the NFL for 11 years before switching to producing and acting. According to ESPN, he joined the Oakland Raiders in 2003 and helped the group win three Pro Bowls. Asomugha switched teams in 2011, leaving the Raiders for the Philadelphia Eagles, where he signed a five-year deal, but was let go after only two seasons.

Shortly after, he began playing for the San Francisco 49ers in 2013, though Asomugha appeared in only three games before the team released him. That same year, he announced his retirement from the NFL. Asomugha and Washington wed in a quiet outdoor ceremony in Idaho in June 2013. According to the reports, the wedding was a top-secret ceremony, and the vows were exchanged at a friend's house. A small private plane carried a select group of guests to a magnificent home. The pair limited who they invited. There were only close family and friends there. People stayed at the house as they made their own vows. It was quite straightforward and nice.

Asomugha and Washington are the parents of three kids. Just a few months before their first wedding anniversary, on April 21, 2014, the couple gave birth to their first child, Isabelle Amarachi. On October 5, 2016, the couple welcomed their son Caleb Kelechi, making Isabelle a big sister.

Kerry was ecstatic to have two children. Her life was drastically improved by having Isabelle, and she was thrilled to grow the family. She does well during pregnancy because she ate well and knows how to take care of her body. The pair also have custody of Asomugha's daughter from an earlier union.

> **Other Relationships**

Despite keeping her personal affairs secret, Washington has talked about the value of maintaining a balance between her personal and professional lives. She has talked about the difficulties of being a working mother and the need to put self-care first. To achieve a healthy work-life balance, Washington emphasizes the significance of setting limits and making time for oneself.

Washington has also been forthright about her political views and activism. She has been a vocal supporter of a number of causes, including racial justice, LGBTQ+ rights, and women's rights. She has actively participated in campaigns and events promoting social justice concerns and has used her platform to spread awareness of these issues.

Outside of her own family, Washington has maintained close contacts with prominent actors and industry colleagues such as Reese Witherspoon. She is also recognized for encouraging and supporting other Hollywood women, and she has given speeches on the value of cooperation and sisterhood.

Washington has been upfront about her dedication to her family, even though she generally keeps her private life out of the spotlight. She frequently posts snippets of her family life on social media and has spoken about the happiness and fulfillment she derives from her roles as a wife and mother.

Kerry Washington has generally preferred to keep her private life private, however she has revealed some information about her family and relationships. She is notable for her dedication to her family, her work as an advocate, and her ability to strike a great work-life balance. Many people find inspiration in her ability to balance her personal and professional life with grace and commitment.

> **Philanthropic Work**

In addition to her success in the entertainment business, Kerry Washington is renowned for her charity efforts and activism. She has supported numerous causes and organizations with the help of her platform and resources while promoting social justice, equality, and female empowerment.

Education is one of Washington's most important issues. She participated in and held an honorary chair position for the

President's Committee on the Arts and Humanities. She worked on this committee to advance arts education and broaden kids' access to the arts nationwide. Washington has worked to ensure that every child has access to a high-quality arts education because she believes in the ability of the arts to encourage creativity, critical thinking, and self-expression.

In addition, Washington has been actively involved in assisting groups that advocate women's and girls' empowerment. She has been a steadfast advocate for the V-Day campaign, which seeks to eradicate violence against women and girls everywhere. She has participated in charitable productions of "The Vagina Monologues" and has used her platform to advocate against gender-based discrimination and violence.

Washington has sponsored several groups that promote women's rights and empowerment in addition to her work with V-Day. She has worked with the Women's Media Centre, a group that promotes gender equality in the media and seeks to highlight women's voices. Washington has advocated for the value of diversity and representation in the media and has utilized her platform to assist and inspire other women working in the field.

She has additionally supported LGBTQ+ rights. She has spoken out against the injustice and discrimination that the LGBTQ+ community has to deal with and has been associated with GLAAD (Gay & Lesbian Alliance Against Defamation). Washington has raised her voice in favor of equal rights for all people because she believes in the value of inclusivity and acceptance.

Washington has utilized her position as an actor in addition to her direct involvement with numerous organizations to raise awareness of significant social concerns. She has addressed issues like politics, race, and social justice through her appearances in films like "American Son" and TV dramas like "Scandal." Washington has used her performances to start conversations and encourage constructive change because she believes in the ability of narrative to foster empathy and understanding.

In general, Kerry Washington's charitable activity demonstrates her dedication to leveraging her platform for good. She has been actively involved in promoting causes that favor social justice, women's rights, education, and LGBTQ+ rights. She has fought for social justice and the empowerment of marginalized groups through her activism. Washington's commitment to philanthropy is evidence of her moral character and her understanding of the value of giving back.

CHAPTER 4

UNIQUE STYLE AND INFLUENCES

➢ Acting Style

Kerry Washington is renowned for her adaptable acting technique, which has enabled her to play a variety of challenging and captivating characters. She displays her talent and versatility as an actress by being able to switch between many genres and characters with ease.

Her ability to portray extreme emotional depth and vulnerability is one of Washington's acting style's defining characteristics. She possesses a unique ability to delve into the feelings of her characters and vividly bring them to life for viewers. Washington provides a feeling of honesty and rawness to her performances, regardless of whether she is portraying a character who is powerful and resolute or one who is weak and tormented.

Washington's rigorous attention to detail is another aspect of her performance that sets her apart. She meticulously considers the subtleties of her characters, painstakingly constructing their physically, speech patterns, and mannerisms. She can thoroughly immerse herself in her parts thanks to her attention to detail, giving them depth and credibility.

Regarding influences, Washington has named a number of performers who have shaped and inspired her career. Cicely Tyson, a legendary actress renowned for her potent performances and dedication to presenting strong Black women on cinema, is one of her main influences. Washington has frequently discussed how Tyson's writing has influenced her own acting style, especially in terms of the value of authenticity and representation.

Denzel Washington, an unrelated actor, is another who has impacted Washington. She has expressed her admiration for his ability to command the screen with his presence and energy as well as how much she has been inspired by his performances. Kerry Washington has been inspired by Denzel Washington's devotion to presenting meaningful stories and his dedication to his art.

Washington has also stated that a variety of actors and actresses, such as Meryl Streep, Viola Davis, and Angela Bassett, serve as inspirations for her work. She respects their abilities, adaptability, and the influence they have had on the business.

It is clear that Kerry Washington draws on both her own special gift and the influences of those who have come before her to create her acting style. She is a known and admired actor in the profession for her ability to give depth, vulnerability, and honesty to her characters. She keeps pushing the envelope and tackling prejudices through her performances, making a lasting impression on both the entertainment business and fans all around the world.

> **Character Development Strategy**

Kerry Washington's approach to character creation is grounded in her dedication to developing multidimensional, real-life characters and an in-depth understanding of her parts. She makes great effort to thoroughly comprehend the motivations, feelings, and emotions of her characters by conducting extensive study and submerging herself in their world.

Washington's painstaking attention to detail is one component of her method for developing characters. She explores the subtleties of her characters, examining their bodily traits, speech patterns, and mannerisms. She is able to give her performances a sense of realism and plausibility by paying meticulous attention to these elements. She can thoroughly embody her characters as a result of her attention to detail, giving them depth and complexity.

Washington places a strong emphasis on comprehending the emotional journey of her characters in addition to paying close attention to the details. She explores their prior traumas, desires, and experiences an effort to comprehend what motivates them and what makes them who they are. She is able to dig into her characters' vulnerabilities and portray their feelings in a way that audiences can relate to by getting to the emotional heart of each one of them.

Washington has a thorough research-based approach to character development. She becomes completely engrossed in the lives of her characters, researching their histories, occupations, and settings. She is able to faithfully reflect the experiences and hardships of her characters, which gives her performances realism and depth.

Washington is also renowned for working intently on character development with both directors and other performers. She respects other people's ideas and viewpoints since she thinks that working together improves a performance's overall quality. She is able to explore various interpretations and approaches to her characters by collaborating closely with her coworkers, which results in a fuller and more nuanced representation.

Another important aspect of Washington's approach to character development is her commitment to representation and authenticity. She strives to portray diverse and complex characters, particularly those that challenge stereotypes and provide a platform for underrepresented voices. She is dedicated to telling stories that are meaningful and impactful, and she uses her platform to advocate for greater diversity and inclusion in the entertainment industry.

Overall, Kerry Washington's approach to character development is characterized by meticulous attention to detail, extensive research, emotional depth, and a commitment to authenticity and representation. Through her dedication to her craft, she consistently delivers performances that are compelling, nuanced, and resonant. She is one of the most renowned and regarded actresses in the business thanks to her approach to character development, and with each new job she accepts, she continues to break through barriers and defy prejudices.

➤ Inspirations and Role Models

Kerry Washington has talked about a number of people during her career who have motivated and acted as role models for her. Cicely Tyson, a renowned actress and civil rights activist, served as one of her initial sources of inspiration. Washington has frequently stated how much she admires Tyson's talent, grace, and use of her position to promote social change. Tyson's dedication to authenticity and her talent for bringing difficult characters to life struck a deep chord with Washington and had an impact on the way she approached acting herself.

Valerie Washington, Washington's mother, has also had a significant impact on her life. Kerry was nurtured with a strong work ethic and a love of learning by Valerie, a professor and educational consultant. She gave Kerry advice on how to follow her aspirations and stressed the value of education and information. Washington's work and morals have greatly benefited from Valerie's support and advice.

Oprah Winfrey and Shonda Rhimes are two additional trailblazing females in the entertainment world whom Washington admires. Washington has been motivated by Winfrey's success as a media tycoon and philanthropist to utilize her platform for good and to elevate underrepresented perspectives. Washington has looked up to Rhimes, the creator of popular dramas including "Grey's Anatomy" and "Scandal," as a mentor and role model. Washington's own professional decisions and advocacy efforts have been affected by Rhimes' commitment to exploring diverse stories and developing multidimensional female characters.

Washington has found inspiration in a variety of artists and activists who have led the road for greater representation in the entertainment business, in addition to these people. She has praised the talent, adaptability, and dedication to conveying significant stories of performers like Denzel Washington, Angela Bassett, and Viola Davis, citing their work as inspiration.

The activism and advocacy of people like Martin Luther King Jr., Rosa Parks, and the Black Lives Matter movement have also had an impact on Washington. She has made use of her platform to speak out against racial injustice and to advance diversity and inclusion in Hollywood because she understands the ability of storytelling to affect social change.

Kerry Washington's motivation to use her ability and platform for good change is reflected in her list of influences and role models. She respects those who have exercised their power to oppose the status quo, elevate underrepresented voices, and promote social justice. Washington continues to break down barriers and have a huge influence on the entertainment business as well as society at large by taking inspiration from these individuals.

CHAPTER 5

FILMOGRAPHY

Washington's filmography is diverse and impressive, showcasing her range as an actress and her ability to tackle complex and compelling roles. She has appeared in a wide variety of films, from dramas to comedies, and has consistently delivered powerful performances that have garnered critical acclaim.

One of Washington's breakout roles came in the 2001 film "Save the Last Dance," where she played Chenille, a supportive friend to the film's protagonist. Her performance in this film showcased her talent for bringing depth and authenticity to her characters, even in supporting roles.

In 2004, Washington starred in the critically acclaimed film "Ray," alongside Jamie Foxx. She portrayed Della Bea Robinson, the wife of Ray Charles. Her performance earned her widespread recognition and praise, and she was nominated for several awards, including a Screen Actors Guild Award for Outstanding Performance by a Cast in a Motion Picture.

Another notable film in Washington's career is "The Last King of Scotland" (2006), where she played Kay Amin, the wife of Ugandan dictator Idi Amin, portrayed by Forest Whitaker. Her performance in this film earned her a nomination for a NAACP Image Award for Outstanding Supporting Actress.

Washington's talent for portraying strong and complex female characters was further showcased in the 2010 drama "For Colored Girls." Directed by Tyler Perry and based on Ntozake Shange's play, the film explored the experiences of African American women. Washington's performance as Kelly, a woman struggling with an abusive relationship, was widely praised for its emotional depth and vulnerability.

In 2012, Washington took on the iconic role of Broomhilda von Shaft in Quentin Tarantino's "Django Unchained." The film tackled the sensitive subject of slavery, and Washington's portrayal of a slave woman seeking freedom showcased her ability to bring strength and resilience to her characters.

However, it was Washington's role as Olivia Pope in the hit television series "Scandal" that truly catapulted her into the spotlight. The show, created by Shonda Rhimes, premiered in 2012 and ran for seven seasons. Washington's portrayal of Pope, a powerful political fixer, earned her widespread acclaim and numerous award nominations. She became the first African American woman to lead a network drama series in over three decades, solidifying her status as a trailblazer in the industry.

In recent years, Washington has continued to take on challenging and impactful roles. She starred in the 2019 drama film "American Son," reprising her role from the Broadway play of the same name. The film explores themes of race, identity, and police brutality, and Washington's performance as a mother searching for answers about her missing son received critical acclaim.

Washington has also ventured into producing, serving as an executive producer on projects such as the HBO film "Confirmation" (2016), where she portrayed Anita Hill, and the Hulu series "Little Fires Everywhere" (2020), based on the novel by Celeste Ng.

Overall, Kerry Washington's filmography is a testament to her talent, versatility, and commitment to telling meaningful stories. From her early breakout roles to her groundbreaking portrayal of Olivia Pope, she has consistently pushed boundaries and made a significant impact in the entertainment industry. Through her performances, Washington continues to challenge stereotypes, uplift underrepresented voices, and advocate for social change.

> ➢ **Television Roles**

Kerry Washington's television roles have been just as diverse and impactful as her filmography. She has proven her versatility and talent through a range of characters, showcasing her ability to tackle complex and compelling roles on the small screen.

Her most notable television role is undoubtedly Olivia Pope in the hit series "Scandal." Premiering in 2012 and running for seven seasons, the show follows Pope, a powerful political fixer who works to protect the reputations of high-profile clients while navigating her own personal and professional challenges. Washington's portrayal of Pope was groundbreaking, as she became the first African American woman to lead a network drama series in over three decades. Her performance earned her widespread acclaim and numerous award nominations, including Primetime Emmy nominations for Outstanding Lead Actress in a Drama Series.

As Olivia Pope, Washington brought a unique blend of intelligence, strength, and vulnerability to the character. She navigated complex political landscapes, handled high-stakes crises, and maintained an air of confidence and control. Washington's chemistry with her co-stars, particularly Tony Goldwyn as President Fitzgerald Grant, added an extra layer of depth to the show. Her portrayal of Pope resonated with audiences, and she became an iconic figure in television history.

In addition to "Scandal," Washington has taken on other memorable television roles. In 2009, she portrayed Anita Hill in the HBO film "Confirmation." The film explores Hill's sexual harassment allegations against Supreme Court nominee Clarence Thomas and the subsequent Senate hearings. Washington's performance as Hill was powerful and nuanced, capturing the emotional turmoil and strength of the real-life figure. Her portrayal earned her critical acclaim and an Emmy nomination for Outstanding Lead Actress in a Limited Series or Movie.

Washington also ventured into producing with the Hulu series "Little Fires Everywhere," based on the novel by Celeste Ng. In addition to starring as Mia Warren, a bohemian artist who becomes entangled with a wealthy suburban family, Washington served as an executive producer on the show. "Little Fires Everywhere" delves into issues of race, class, motherhood, and identity, and Washington's performance was praised for its complexity and depth. The series further demonstrated her commitment to telling meaningful stories and amplifying underrepresented voices.

Throughout her television career, Washington has consistently chosen roles that challenge stereotypes and push boundaries. She has been a trailblazer for representation and diversity in the industry, using her platform to advocate for social change. Her performances have captivated audiences and garnered critical acclaim, solidifying her status as one of the most talented and influential actresses in television today.

In summary, Kerry Washington's television roles, particularly her portrayal of Olivia Pope in "Scandal," have made a significant impact on the small screen. Her talent, versatility, and commitment to telling meaningful stories shine through in each character she embodies. Washington continues to break barriers, challenge stereotypes, and uplift underrepresented voices, leaving a lasting legacy in the television industry.

> ### Film Roles

Kerry Washington's filmography is equally as impressive and impactful as her television roles. Throughout her career, she has taken on a wide range of characters, showcasing her versatility and talent in the world of cinema.

One of Washington's most notable film roles is that of Ray Charles' wife, Della Bea Robinson, in the biographical drama "Ray" (2004). The film tells the story of the legendary musician and his rise to fame, as well as his struggles with drug addiction and personal relationships. Washington's portrayal of Della Bea was heartfelt and nuanced, capturing the strength and resilience of a woman who stood by her husband through thick and thin. Her performance earned her critical acclaim and a nomination for Best Supporting Actress at the NAACP Image Awards.

In 2010, Washington starred alongside Jamie Foxx in the crime thriller "Django Unchained," directed by Quentin Tarantino. The film takes place in the antebellum South and follows a freed slave named Django as he teams up with a bounty hunter to rescue his wife from a cruel plantation owner. Washington portrayed Broomhilda von Shaft, Django's wife, with grace and vulnerability. Her performance added depth to the character and highlighted the emotional toll of slavery. "Django Unchained" received widespread acclaim, and Washington's performance was praised for its emotional impact.

Washington also explored the world of political drama in the film "The Last King of Scotland" (2006). Starring alongside Forest Whitaker, she played Kay Amin, the wife of Ugandan dictator Idi

Amin. The film delves into Amin's brutal regime and the effect it has on those around him. Washington's portrayal of Kay showcased her ability to navigate complex emotions and captivate audiences with her performance. Her work in "The Last King of Scotland" earned her nominations for Best Supporting Actress at the BAFTA Awards and the Screen Actors Guild Awards.

In addition to these notable roles, Washington has taken on a variety of other film projects, including the romantic comedy "Save the Last Dance" (2001), the crime thriller "Lakeview Terrace" (2008), and the historical drama "The Immortal Life of Henrietta Lacks" (2017). In each of these films, Washington's talent and dedication to her craft shine through, elevating the stories and characters she brings to life.

Beyond her individual performances, Washington has also been involved in producing and advocating for diverse storytelling in the film industry. She co-produced and starred in the drama film "American Son" (2019), which tackles issues of race and police brutality. The film premiered on Netflix and received critical acclaim for its powerful and thought-provoking narrative.

Overall, Kerry Washington's film roles have been just as diverse and impactful as her television roles. She has consistently chosen projects that challenge stereotypes, push boundaries, and shed light on important social issues. Washington's talent, versatility, and commitment to telling meaningful stories have solidified her status as one of the most talented and influential actresses in both television and film.

CHAPTER 6

BEHIND THE SCENE

While there is limited public information available about Kerry Washington's personal life behind the scenes, she is known to be a private individual who prefers to keep her personal details out of the public eye. However, in this response, I will discuss some general aspects of Kerry Washington's work ethic, passion for her craft, and her commitment to creating positive change in the entertainment industry.

Kerry Washington is renowned for her exceptional work ethic and dedication to her craft. Co-stars, directors, and colleagues often speak highly of her professionalism, preparedness, and collaborative spirit on set. Known for her strong commitment to her characters, Washington invests significant time and effort into research and preparation, ensuring her performances carries depth and authenticity.

Washington's commitment to her roles extends beyond just her individual performance. She actively engages with the creative process, seeking opportunities for collaboration and offering valuable insights to enhance the projects she works on. She has been involved in developing storylines, and she has served as a producer on various projects, leveraging her influence to create meaningful storytelling that pushes boundaries and promotes inclusivity.

While behind the scenes, Washington actively advocates for greater diversity and representation in the entertainment industry. She recognizes the importance of using her platform and voice to effect change and challenge existing structures. Washington has been vocal about the need for more opportunities and better representation for women, people of color, and other marginalized communities. Her stance has brought attention to the industry's shortcomings and sparked conversations about inclusivity in Hollywood.

Beyond her work on-screen, Washington promotes social justice and civic engagement. She has been involved in various philanthropic efforts and uses her platform to raise awareness of social issues, leveraging her influence to support causes she is passionate about. Whether it is advocating for civil liberties, speaking out against inequality, or lending support to grassroots organizations, Washington actively uses her celebrity status for positive change.

In addition to her professional steadfastness, Kerry Washington values maintaining a level of privacy in her personal life. She tends to keep her personal relationships and family life out of the public eye, focusing instead on her craft and using her platform to uplift marginalized voices and promote social progress.

Kerry Washington's commitment to her craft, dedication to creating positive change, and preference for privacy behind the scenes contribute to her reputation as a highly respected and influential figure in the entertainment industry. Her work ethic, collaborative spirit, and advocacy efforts shine through in her performances, her production work, and her engagement with social issues. Kerry Washington continues to be an inspiring figure who uses her talent and influence to make a difference both on and off-screen.

➤ A Producer And Director

While Kerry Washington is primarily known for her remarkable acting career, she has also made significant strides in producing and directing projects that prioritize diverse storytelling and amplify underrepresented voices. In this response, I will delve extensively into Washington's work as a producer and director, exploring her contributions, motivations, and impact on the entertainment industry.

As a producer, Washington has been instrumental in championing diverse storytelling and promoting inclusive narratives. She established her production company, Simpson Street, with a mission to develop and produce projects that uplift underrepresented voices and challenge existing narratives.

Through Simpson Street, Washington has demonstrated a commitment to working on projects that tackle pertinent social issues, amplify marginalized perspectives, and offer fresh storytelling. She has been involved in producing projects across multiple mediums, including television, film, and stage.

One notable project Washington produced was the HBO film "Confirmation" (2016), in which she also starred as the lead character, Anita Hill. The film explores Hill's experiences during the controversial Senate confirmation hearings for Supreme Court Justice Clarence Thomas. "Confirmation" received critical acclaim for its nuanced exploration of gender dynamics, racial politics, and the importance of elevating women's voices.

In addition to producing, Washington has also directed episodes of television series, showcasing her talent behind the camera. She has lent her directorial skills to shows such as "Scandal," the series in which she starred, and "Insecure." Her passion for directing stems

41

from a desire to engage with the creative process on a deeper level and shape narratives from a different perspective.

Washington's involvement as a producer and director aligns with her broader commitment to advocating for representation and diversity within the entertainment industry. She uses her influence and platform to carve out opportunities for underrepresented groups, both in front of and behind the camera. By spearheading projects that prioritize diverse storytelling, Washington helps foster an inclusive and equitable industry where a wider range of voices can be heard.

Through her producing and directing endeavors, Washington seeks to challenge prevailing narratives, break down barriers, and create a more inclusive entertainment landscape. Her work contributes to the ongoing discussions and efforts aimed at increasing representation, breaking stereotypes, and amplifying underrepresented stories.

Furthermore, Washington's involvement as a producer and director serves as an inspiration and example for aspiring artists from marginalized communities. Her accomplishments highlight the importance of not only being in front of the camera but also actively participating in the decision-making processes that shape the stories being told.

In conclusion, Kerry Washington's foray into producing and directing projects speaks to her dedication to diversity, representation, and the power of storytelling. Through her production company, Simpson Street, she actively seeks out projects that elevate underrepresented voices, challenge societal norms, and shed light on pressing social issues. Washington's involvement as a producer and director not only uplifts the projects she is a part of but also has a broader impact in reshaping the landscape of the entertainment industry.

➤ Advocate Of Diversity And Inclusion

Kerry Washington has been at the forefront of advocating for diversity and inclusion in Hollywood, using her influence and platform to effect tangible change within the industry. In this response, I will delve extensively into Kerry Washington's advocacy work, exploring her efforts to promote representation, challenge stereotypes, and champion inclusivity in the entertainment industry.

Washington has been a vocal advocate for increased diversity and equal opportunities for underrepresented communities, both in front of and behind the camera. She has used her prominent platform to raise awareness and address the disparities that exist within the industry, calling for greater representation and more inclusive narratives.

One of Washington's key contributions to advocacy has been her involvement in conversations surrounding the portrayal of women, especially women of color, in media. She has consistently challenged narrow and stereotypical portrayals, highlighting the importance of complex, fully realized characters that reflect the diversity of human experiences. Washington advocates for well-rounded roles that showcase the multitude of talents, abilities, and narratives that exist within marginalized communities.

Additionally, Washington has called for increased representation of women and people of color in influential positions within the industry, such as writers, directors, producers, and executives. She has highlighted the significance of having diverse voices in decision-making roles, as they shape the stories told and the perspectives offered. Washington emphasizes that inclusion in these positions is necessary for authentic storytelling and for dismantling systemic barriers that limit opportunities for marginalized communities.

In her advocacy work, Washington has participated in industry-wide initiatives focused on promoting diversity and inclusion. For instance, she was involved in the creation of the Frances McDormand-led "inclusion rider" movement, which encourages the inclusion of more diverse talent both on-screen and behind the scenes. Washington's dedication to ensuring equal representation and diverse storytelling has created ripples of change, sparking conversations and inspiring others in the industry.

Outside of Hollywood, Washington has been actively engaged in political and social activism. She uses her platform to draw attention to social justice issues and advocate for equality and inclusivity in various spheres of society. Her commitment to the betterment of marginalized communities extends beyond her on-screen work, demonstrating a deep understanding of the intersectionality between activism, representation, and media representation.

Through her advocacy for diversity and inclusion, Kerry Washington has become a role model and an inspiration for aspiring actors, filmmakers, and advocates. Her consistent calls for change and her dedication to creating opportunities for underrepresented voices have helped shape the discourse surrounding representation in the entertainment industry.

In conclusion, Kerry Washington's advocacy work within Hollywood has had a substantial impact on the ongoing conversations surrounding diversity and inclusion in the industry.

By championing increased representation, challenging stereotypes, and using her platform to amplify marginalized voices, Washington has played a pivotal role in driving change. Her relentless efforts to promote a more inclusive and equitable Hollywood help paved the way for a more representative and authentically diverse entertainment landscape.

KERRY WASHINGTON BIO

CHAPTER 7

IMPACT AND LEGACY

Kerry Washington is a renowned and extremely prominent actress who has had a big impact on the entertainment business. She has received a great deal of praise and recognition over the course of her career for her extraordinary talent, adaptability, and dedication to telling stories that subvert social norms and advance inclusivity. Beyond her on-screen roles, Washington has made a significant contribution to society by championing diversity in Hollywood, empowering women, and social justice issues.

Particularly in the ground-breaking television series "Scandal," Kerry Washington's ability to portray characters that are complicated and multidimensional is one of her most lasting contributions. She made history by being the first African-American female lead in a primetime network drama in more than 40 years when she played Olivia Pope. Washington's portrayal of the bold and courageous crisis management specialist resonated with viewers all across the world, cementing her place as an industry trendsetter.

Washington's ability to give her characters depth and nuance has consistently pushed the bounds of representation on television and movies. She has underlined the importance of diverse stories and characters that defy preconceptions and break through boundaries through her performances. Washington has smashed the confining tropes commonly imposed on women of color in mainstream media by showing powerful, clever, and energetic women.

Furthermore, Kerry Washington's influence can be evident through her advocacy and activism. She regularly uses her platform to advocate social change and increase awareness. Washington has been a prominent supporter of civil rights, LGBTQ+ rights, and gender equality. She has actively participated in movements addressing systematic racism, voter suppression, and police brutality, bringing attention to important concerns and pushing others to act.

Washington's involvement in efforts such as the #TimesUp and #MeToo campaigns demonstrates her dedication to empowering women. She has spoken out against sexual harassment and fought for more secure and welcoming workplaces in the entertainment business. She has also advocated for equitable chances for women in top positions in Hollywood and elsewhere.

She has also worked relentlessly as a producer to provide opportunities for minority perspectives. Simpson Street, her production firm, has produced films that elevate varied viewpoints and narratives. She continues to create a lasting impact on the industry by aggressively searching out and supporting rising talent and establishing an inclusive and representative entertainment scene.

Kerry Washington's legacy is defined by her unrivaled talent, dedication to social justice, and support for diversity and inclusion. She has been an inspiration for young performers and campaigners alike, thanks to her stunning performances and steadfast advocacy. Her impact goes far beyond the entertainment business, as she continues to use her voice and platform to effect positive change and construct a more equal society.

> **Breaking Through Barriers**

As a Black female leader in the entertainment industry, Kerry Washington has played a critical part in bringing down barriers and smashing glass ceilings. Throughout her career, she has challenged cultural standards and fought against the lack of representation of women of color on screen, leaving an indelible mark on Hollywood and inspiring future generations.

Black women as leading characters in mainstream culture have long been underrepresented. Kerry Washington's breakout performance as Olivia Pope in the blockbuster television series "Scandal" was a watershed moment in television history. Washington disrupted the conventional narrative by playing a bright, powerful, and sophisticated heroine who takes center stage, proving that women of color can lead successful primetime network dramas.

Washington's portrayal of Olivia Pope, the first African-American female lead in a network drama in more than 40 years, gave Black women on television much-needed prominence and representation. She not only attracted audiences globally by breaking down the bounds of traditional casting practices, but she also served as a symbol of development and inclusivity in the entertainment industry.

Washington's portrayal of Olivia Pope did more than only break down barriers; it also destroyed stereotypes of Black women. Olivia Pope is a dynamic heroine with her own agency who is not constrained to the limited roles that Black women on TV are frequently allotted. Washington instilled depth, intelligence, and complexity into Olivia Pope through her painstaking portrayal, challenging preconceived conceptions and demolishing detrimental stereotypes.

Kerry Washington led the charge in "Scandal," not only paving the door for more diverse tales and characters but also inspiring other

Black actors to pursue leading roles. She proved that women of color can carry narratives, captivate viewers, and propel television shows and films to success.

Washington's influence as a Black female leader transcends her own efforts. She has emerged as a formidable advocate for inclusion and diversity in Hollywood, utilizing her platform to campaign for increased opportunities for marginalized voices. She has been outspoken on the significance of equal representation both in front of and behind the camera, and she has worked hard to provide opportunities for marginalized people in the business.

Furthermore, Kerry Washington's triumph as a Black female protagonist has reverberated throughout the industry. It has made it possible to tell more varied tales and has encouraged the industry to broaden its perspectives and accept marginalized voices. Washington's influence and accomplishments have acted as an inspiration to Black performers and creators, encouraging them to pursue their dreams and tell tales that appeal to viewers of all backgrounds.

In conclusion, Kerry Washington's emergence as a Black female lead in Hollywood has been groundbreaking. She has broken through barriers, challenged preconceptions, and advocated for greater diversity and inclusivity through her compelling performances. Her influence extends beyond her own achievement, as she has cleared the path for more Black women to play prominent roles and has emerged as a powerful advocate for change in Hollywood. Kerry Washington's legacy will continue to inspire and uplift future generations of actors and storytellers, helping to shape a more diverse and inclusive entertainment business.

Pop Culture Influence and Representation

Kerry Washington has had a tremendous and far-reaching impact on pop culture and representation. She has made a lasting impact on the entertainment business as an outstanding actor, advocate, and producer, defying conventional standards and encouraging diverse and inclusive representation.

Kerry Washington's notable performances in both television and movies have had a significant impact on pop culture. Her portrayal of nuanced and powerful characters, particularly in the highly acclaimed series "Scandal," has captivated audiences across the world and contributed to a shift in how women of color are portrayed on film. Washington's ability to bring depth, intelligence, and sensitivity to her characters has called into question established preconceptions and opened up new avenues for representation.

Washington's performances proved that women of color can dominate not only in terms of on-screen presence but also in their capacity to carry the narrative and drive project success. Her popularity has cleared the path for other actors of color to win starring roles, and she has been instrumental in diversifying the tales and characters we see in popular culture.

Kerry Washington has been an ardent advocate for representation and inclusivity in Hollywood, in addition to her on-screen presence. She has aggressively used her platform as a prominent voice to promote the need for more varied storytelling, better chances for marginalized populations, and equitable representation in front of and behind the camera. She has helped bring attention to the structural difficulties faced by underrepresented groups in the industry by her advocacy and participation in campaigns such as Time's Up and #OscarsSoWhite.

Washington's influence has extended beyond Hollywood. Her influence on pop culture extends beyond her status as a fashion icon. She has solidified herself as a trendsetter and has inspired numerous individuals to embrace their own distinctive style and express themselves authentically. She is known for her excellent sense of style and red-carpet appearance.

Furthermore, Kerry Washington's prominence as a producer has allowed her to actively affect the landscape of popular culture representation. She has been active in projects that prioritize diverse storytelling and elevate marginalized perspectives as the co-founder of Simpson Street Productions. She has offered possibilities for narratives and talent that would otherwise go unnoticed by financing and producing productions that celebrate underrepresented communities.

Washington has become a role model for young performers, writers, and spectators alike with her combination of talent, activism, and production work. Her effect on pop culture has promoted a sense of confidence and pride in previously marginalized populations. She has played an important role in reframing the debate around diversity and inclusion in the industry by questioning the established quo and demanding better representation.

In conclusion, Kerry Washington's impact on pop culture and representation cannot be overstated. She has broken down barriers, questioned preconceptions and advocated for more inclusive and varied storytelling through her performances, advocacy, and production work. Her effect goes beyond her personal success or individual projects because she has inspired a new generation of artists, and her influence will continue to alter the industry for years to come. The dedication to representation shown by Kerry

Washington serves as a reminder of the media's revolutionary potential in building a more just and inclusive society.

CHAPTER 8

Washington has received countless awards and honors, which are a testament to her talent and contributions to the entertainment business. She is a well-known actress who has won awards and garnered praise for her outstanding work in a variety of disciplines, including theatre, cinema, and television.

Washington received a lot of acclaim and nominations for many awards for her depiction of Olivia Pope in the popular television series "Scandal." She got three nominations for Primetime Emmy Awards in the category of Outstanding Lead Actress in a Drama Series, making history as the first African-American woman to do so in 20 years. She didn't receive an Emmy, but her outstanding performance in "Scandal" cemented her place among the biggest names in television.

Washington has received several significant honors for her depiction as Olivia Pope in addition to the Primetime Emmy recognition. She was nominated for an Outstanding Performance by a Female Actor in a Drama Series Screen Actors Guild (SAG) Award. She also received the BET Award for Best Actress and the Television Critics Association Award for Individual Achievement in Drama.

Washington's significant cinema performances serve as proof that her skill transcends television. She received a lot of praise from critics for her performance in the intense drama "Ray" and was nominated for multiple awards. She was nominated for the NAACP Image Award for Outstanding Supporting Actress in a

Motion Picture as well as the Screen Actors Guild Award for Outstanding Performance by a Female Actor in a Supporting Role.

Additionally acknowledged and praised is Washington's commanding onstage presence. She was nominated for a Drama Desk Award for Outstanding Actress in a Play for her stirring performance in "Race" on Broadway. This honor emphasizes her acting versatility and ability to give strong performances in a variety of settings.

Kerry Washington has been acknowledged for her contributions to the entertainment world in addition to her individual performances. She has established her effect and influence outside of the acting industry by being named one of Time magazine's 100 Most Influential People in the World. Washington has additionally been honored with numerous NAACP Image Awards for Outstanding Actress in a Drama Series, a testament to her unwavering quality and contributions to the industry.

The dedication of Washington to activism and campaigning has also not gone unnoticed. She has received the GLAAD Vanguard Award in recognition of her work to advance LGBTQ+ acceptance and her support of the group. For her efforts to advance social justice and advocate for inclusive representation, she also won the Chairman's Award at the NAACP Image Awards.

In conclusion, Kerry Washington has received recognition and admiration for her work throughout her career due to her talent and commitment to her art. She has continuously pushed boundaries and produced excellent work, from her ground-breaking part in "Scandal" to her memorable performances in film and theatre. In addition to recognizing her skill, Washington has received honors, nominations, and recognitions that also recognize her contributions as a trailblazer for minority representation in the entertainment industry. Her contributions have had a lasting impression and

56

continue to motivate audiences and other artists. We shall delve extensively into these honors to learn more about Kerry's exploits that merit recognition.

> ➢ **Emmy Awards**

Kerry Washington has received numerous Emmy nominations over her career, has had a major influence on the television industry. Although she has yet to get an Emmy, her work and talents have cemented her reputation as one of the most accomplished and well-respected actresses in the business.

Washington won a lot of praise for her depiction of Olivia Pope in the popular television programs "Scandal." She received many nominations for Outstanding Lead Actress in a Drama Series at the Primetime Emmys thanks to her remarkable acting abilities and capacity to give her characters depth and complexity.

For her work in "Scandal's" second season, Washington received her first Primetime Emmy nomination in 2013. She was the first African-American woman to be nominated in the Lead Actress in a Drama Series category in more than ten years, which was a significant turning point. Her nomination was as a testament to both her outstanding performance and the effect of her portrayal of Olivia Pope as a tenacious, perceptive, and complex figure.

Washington continued to dazzle audiences and reviewers alike in the years that followed, winning additional Emmy nods for her performance in "Scandal." Her ability to convey emotion, command the screen, and navigate complex storylines showcased her outstanding talent and solidified her as one of the most dynamic actresses on television.

Washington's Emmy nominations not only recognized her individual achievement but also highlighted the groundbreaking representation she brought to the small screen. As an influential figure for women of color, her presence and recognition at the Emmy Awards served as a testament to the need for diverse representation and opened the door for more inclusive narratives in television.

While Washington has yet to take home an Emmy award, her significant contributions and impact on the industry cannot be understated. Her nominations alone speak volumes about her talent and the respect she has garnered within the television community. It is impossible to ignore the cultural impact of her character's image because of how well-known her portrayal of Olivia Pope has become.

It is also important to remember that Washington's numerous accomplishments and contributions to the entertainment industry go far beyond just winning Emmys. She has aggressively promoted diversity, inclusivity, and equal representation in Hollywood, thus her influence goes beyond accolades. Washington continues to advocate for structural change within the business through her work as a producer and her involvement in program supporting underrepresented voices, opening doors for disadvantaged groups and fostering a more inclusive entertainment scene.

Kerry Washington has received multiple nominations, demonstrating both her extraordinary talent and the substantial contribution she has made to television, even though she has yet to win an Emmy. Her portrayal of Olivia Pope in "Scandal" changed the way prominent women were portrayed on television and provided much-needed representation. Washington's influence goes beyond accolades since she is still a trailblazer in the industry for advancing diversity and inclusiveness. Future generations of

58

actors and producers will definitely be motivated by her legacy to pursue greatness, authenticity, and representation in television and other media.

> ### ➤ Golden Globe Awards

Kerry Washington, a gifted and well-known actress, has been nominated for numerous Golden Globe Awards in recognition of her great work in the entertainment business. Her outstanding performances and contributions have cemented her place as one of the industry's most renowned and celebrated figures, despite the fact that she has yet to win a Golden Globe.

Washington has received praise from critics and numerous Golden Globe nominations for her notable performances in both television and movies. The role of Olivia Pope she played in the popular television series "Scandal" propelled her into the public eye and made her a formidable force. She received nominated for Best Actress in a Television Series - Drama because of her talent for bringing complexity, strength, and vulnerability to the role.

Washington was nominated for her first Golden Globe in 2013 for her performance in "Scandal." She was the first African-American woman to be nominated in the main acting category for a television drama in nearly two decades thanks to this historic milestone. Her nomination not only acknowledged her extraordinary talent but also emphasized the need for greater diversity in the profession.

Washington continued to enthrall viewers with her outstanding performances in the ensuing years, winning additional Golden Globe nominations for her work in "Scandal." Each nomination demonstrated her ability to command the screen and develop complex characters, reiterating her standing as one of television's most engaging and renowned performers.

Washington received Golden Globe nods for her work in films including "Ray" and "Django Unchained" in addition to television. These roles demonstrated her acting talent and adaptability, showing that she could play a variety of complex characters in different genres.

Washington has been nominated for numerous Golden Globes, despite the fact that she has yet to win one. This speaks volumes about her brilliance and the impact she has had on the business. She received Golden Globe honors. In addition to showcasing her particular accomplishments, awards have drawn attention to the value of varied representation and the demand for more inclusive storytelling.

Washington's accomplishments go beyond her on-screen appearances and go beyond her nominations and awards. She has actively promoted diversity and inclusion and utilized her platform to call for equitable representation in Hollywood. Her work as a producer and her participation in movements like Time's Up and #OscarsSoWhite show how dedicated she is to bringing about structural change and opening doors for voices that are marginalized.

Kerry Washington has had multiple nominations, demonstrating both her extraordinary talent and the impact she has had on the entertainment business, even though she has yet to win a Golden Globe. She has cemented her reputation as one of television's most formidable actors because to her performances in "Scandal" and other significant ventures. Washington continues to pioneer the road for diversity and inclusiveness in Hollywood, so her influence goes beyond accolades. Future generations of performers and producers are motivated and empowered by her truthful representations and advocacy work to fight for representation and social change in the entertainment business.

➤ Screen Actors Guild Awards

Kerry Washington, a seasoned and versatile actress, has received praise for her outstanding work in both television and cinema, earning her numerous Screen Actors Guild (SAG) Award nominations. She has cemented her position as one of the most renowned and recognized actors in the entertainment business with her extraordinary talent and contributions.

Washington received a lot of praise and received multiple SAG Award nominations for her depiction of Olivia Pope in the popular television show "Scandal." Her outstanding acting skills and ability to enthrall audiences throughout the world were demonstrated by the depth, nuance, and emotional range she was able to bring to her character.

Washington was nominated for a SAG Award for Outstanding Performance by a Female Actor in a Drama Series in 2013 for her work in "Scandal." This nomination served as a significant acknowledgement of her extraordinary talent and the significance of her Olivia Pope depiction. Her capacity to embrace a complex character and infuse authenticity into her performances was underlined by this.

Washington continued to impress in the following years, garnering more SAG Award nominations. Her continual success at the SAG Awards highlighted her position as one of the most renowned actors in television and confirmed her talent for giving strong, impactful performances.

61

Washington's abilities go beyond television; her cinema roles have also been nominated for SAG Awards. Her performances in lauded films like "Ray" and "Django Unchained" showcased her versatility and the variety of characters she is capable of authentically portraying.

Washington has not yet taken home a SAG Award, but her nomination show how much the profession values and appreciates the contribution she has made as an actress. These nominations are a prestigious honor in the industry because the SAG Awards honor excellent performances by actors.

Washington has been a part of the award-winning cast of "Scandal," which has received numerous SAG Award nominations for Outstanding Performance by an Ensemble in a Drama Series, in addition to receiving individual acclaim. These nominations further recognize Washington's contributions as a crucial component of the show's success and showcase the talent and chemistry among the show's actors.

Washington has been a strong supporter of diversity and inclusion in the entertainment business in addition to her nominations and awards. She has participated in campaigns promoting underrepresented voices and utilized her position to draw attention to significant social concerns. Her dedication to encouraging constructive change in the industry serves as an example to both her coworkers and followers.

In a nutshell Kerry Washington's numerous SAG Award nominations demonstrate both her outstanding talent and the contribution she has made to the television and film industries. Her portrayal of Olivia Pope in "Scandal" captured viewers' attention and cemented her reputation as one of the field's most admired performers. Washington's nominations highlight her outstanding performances and contributions to the acting industry, despite the fact that she has not yet won a SAG Award. Her efforts and work have had a long-lasting influence on the business, opening the way for varied representation and profound storytelling.

> ### Other Significant Awards

In addition to her recognition at the Primetime Emmy Awards, Golden Globe Awards, and Screen Actors Guild (SAG) Awards, Kerry Washington is a highly successful and well-respected actress who has won a number of other noteworthy awards. Numerous professional organizations and reviewers alike have acknowledged her talent and commitment to her job.

The NAACP Image Award is one major honor Washington has received. Throughout her career, she has received numerous NAACP Image Awards in a variety of categories, including Entertainer of the Year, Outstanding Actress in a Drama Series, and Outstanding Supporting Actress in a Motion Picture. Her exceptional contributions to the entertainment business and her portrayal of African-American brilliance are highlighted by these honors.

Additionally, Washington has received praise from the Critics' Choice Television Awards. She was nominated for Best Actress in a Drama Series for her outstanding performance in "Scandal" The Broadcast Television Journalists Association presents the Critics' Choice Television Awards to honor outstanding television programming.

Washington has also received recognition from the Hollywood Film Awards. She was honored with the Hollywood Supporting

Actress Award for her performance in the widely praised movie "Django Unchained." This honor emphasizes her skill and adaptability as an actor in the movie business and reaffirms her capacity to shine in a variety of roles and genres.

Washington has received individual honors in addition to recognition for her work as a producer in the field of storytelling. She was nominated for an Outstanding Producer of Episodic Television, Drama Producers Guild Award for her work on "Scandal." Her engagement behind the scenes and her commitment to creating intriguing stories are highlighted by this nomination.

Washington has won honorary recognition for her contributions to the profession in addition to specific prizes. She has been recognized as one of the 100 most important persons in the world by Time magazine, demonstrating her considerable influence both on and off the screen. Her advocacy for diversity, inclusivity, and social change within the entertainment business is recognized by this honor.

In conclusion, Washington has consistently received praise and recognition for her accomplishments across a range of award platforms, which highlights her great talent and major contributions to the television and film industries. She has established herself as one of the most revered actors and trailblazers in the business thanks to her continuing success and influence. Washington has made a lasting impression on the world through her performances, activism, and commitment to encouraging diversity representation, inspiring future generations and shaping the landscape of storytelling.

CHAPTER 9

THE SUCCESS CONTINUES

Kerry's incredible skill, adaptability, and unrelenting devotion to her art are the main reasons for her ongoing success in the entertainment world. She is a well-known actress who routinely gives strong performances that attract audiences and win her praise from the critics. Washington has a number of intriguing upcoming projects that promise to broaden her range and establish her as one of Hollywood's most powerful performers.

The Ryan Murphy film "The Prom," which is based on the popular Broadway musical of the same name, is one of Washington's completed projects. It was released in 2020. Meryl Streep, Nicole Kidman, James Corden, and others appear alongside Washington in this musical comedy-drama. The plot revolves around a group of Broadway stars who rally around a small-town lesbian student who wants to accompany her lover to the prom. Washington's participation in this star-studded endeavor demonstrates her capacity to take on varied positions and interact with prominent industry figures.

Another major project that Washington completed recently was the film "The School for Good and Evil," which was released in 2022 and is based on Soman Chainani's popular young adult fantasy literature. Washington not only stars in the film, but she also serves as a producer, demonstrating her dedication to bringing compelling stories to the big screen. This project showcases her ability to navigate different genres and expand her creative involvement behind the scenes.

Additionally, through her production firm, Simpson Street, Washington has dabbled in the area of producing and developing projects. She wants to tell gripping stories through this project that will amplify the perspectives of those who are marginalized and advance diversity and inclusion in the field. Washington continues to influence the direction of entertainment by advocating significant themes that connect with viewers. She does this out of her passion for meaningful storytelling and her dedication to social change.

The theatre has benefited greatly from Washington's accomplishments, and her success goes beyond the screen. She made her Broadway debut in the play "American Son," which looked at issues of race, identity, and police brutality, in 2018. Washington's impressive performance won her praise from the critics and further demonstrated her aptitude for taking on challenging and socially significant issues. Her participation in the play displays her dedication to using her platform to raise awareness of crucial topics and elicit discussions that result in good change.

Kerry Washington's upcoming endeavors and projects will surely continue to have an impact on the industry as an actress, producer, and advocate. Her corpus of work is a testament to her commitment to presenting different people, advocating for inclusivity, and breaking down barriers. Washington contributes to reshaping Hollywood's landscape by repeatedly deciding to work on projects that question social norms and highlight minority narratives, and she encourages others to follow her lead.

Kerry Washington's tremendous talent, adaptability, and love of meaningful storytelling are the reasons for her continued success. She has recently worked on films like "The Prom" and "The School for Good and Evil," showcasing her versatility in roles and genres while working with industry heavyweights. Furthermore, Washington's dedication to campaigning and her work as a producer demonstrate her resolve to highlight overlooked tales. In the future, Washington's professional path is expected to be characterized by provocative performances, socially conscious endeavors, and a persistent dedication to bringing about constructive change in the entertainment sector.

➤ Career Highlights

Kerry Washington has had a truly extraordinary career in the entertainment sector. She has consistently shown her exceptional aptitude, adaptability, and dedication to perfection in whatever she has done, from her early responsibilities to her current endeavors.

One of the most admired and significant actors of her time, her career have demonstrated her unwavering commitment to her profession.

Washington's talent for giving each character she plays depth and subtlety is one of its most noticeable features. She is incredibly talented at losing herself in her characters, giving each one a ton of sincerity and emotion, whether it be on stage or in front of the camera. She has successfully played a variety of roles because to her outstanding talent, including the obstinate Olivia Pope in "Scandal" and the complicated and charismatic Broomhilda von Shaft in "Django Unchained." Washington has often shown her ability to represent characters with nuance, complexity, and humanity while still leaving an impression on viewers.

Her dedication to encouraging diversity and inclusiveness in the industry is another achievement in her career. Both in front of and behind the camera, she has been an outspoken supporter of equal representation. She actively seeks out and develops projects through her production company, Simpson Street, that highlight marginalized perspectives, ensuring that varied stories are given the platform they merit. Her commitment to leveraging her power for the industry's benefit has served as an example to others and paved the path for a more inclusive future.

She has not just succeeded by acting independently. She has dabbled in production, taking on support roles for initiatives that share her ideals and helping to develop narratives. She has been able to further contribute to the industry as well as explore new storytelling horizons thanks to the increase of her creative toolkit.

Washington's influence also goes beyond her professional accomplishments. By supporting causes like LGBTQ+ rights, racial justice, and women's emancipation, she has advocated for causes and used her position to spread awareness about significant social concerns. She has earned respect both inside and outside the entertainment industry for her willingness to speak out on these issues.

Finally, Kerry Washington's career is proof of her enormous talent, adaptability, and commitment. She stands out as an industry trailblazer due to her talent for bringing characters to life, dedication to advancing diversity, and advocacy for social change. Beyond honors and prizes, Washington's influence extends to inspiring other actors and fans all across the world. She continues to influence the direction of the entertainment business with her unwavering dedication to storytelling, representation, and starting important discussions, making a lasting impression on the fields of activism, film, and television.

CONCLUSION

Kerry Washington's career has been nothing short of extraordinary, to sum it up. She has consistently shown her brilliance, adaptability, and tenacity in everything she has done, from her early days in theatre to her ground-breaking roles in film and television. Washington gives her all to every part she takes on, giving compelling performances that enthrall viewers and win critical accolades.

Washington has contested established Hollywood conventions and fought for more inclusive and diverse storytelling throughout her career. Her dedication to championing the interests of marginalized groups and underrepresented voices is evident not only in the roles she selects but also in her advocacy work and production company, Simpson Street. Racial inequality, women's rights, and LGBTQ+ representation are just a few of the pressing social concerns she has brought to light through her platform.

Beyond acting, Washington has made contributions to the entertainment sector. She avidly seeks for projects as producers that pushes boundaries and promote various narratives. Her production firm, Simpson Street, has developed into a platform for inclusive storytelling and the telling of stories that matter.

Washington's peers, critics, and esteemed awards agencies have also taken notice of her influence. Her various honors, which also include Primetime Emmy Awards, Golden Globe Awards, NAACP Image Awards, and Screen Actors Guild Awards, are proof of her talent and the esteem she enjoys in the business.

Washington is a role model and an inspiration to many people in addition to her professional successes. She is revered both on and off the screen thanks to her grace, intelligence, and commitment for social change. She has pushed for a more equal and inclusive entertainment industry by using her position to start important debates.

Kerry Washington's career will undoubtedly continue to grow in the future. She will have a lasting impact in the years to come thanks to her ability to select engaging projects, give outstanding performances, and contribute to significant storytelling. Washington's presence will surely influence the business and provide doors for upcoming generations of artists, whether through her acting, producing, or advocacy work.

Since she is a private person, not much is known about her inner life. Fortunately, the 25th of September saw the publication of Kerry Washington's autobiography, *Thicker Than Water*. She revealed the most intimate details of her life, including the difficulties she faced as a black child growing up in a white neighborhood, her family's upbringing, her eating disorders and addiction, the truth about her paternity, her sexuality, her secret marriage to her husband and other relationships, as well as her accomplishments.

Kerry Washington's life story, in its entirety, is a monument to her brilliance, enthusiasm, and commitment to expanding the possibilities of storytelling. Her career serves as inspiration for aspiring entertainers, serving as a reminder of the importance of using one's platform for positive change. Kerry Washington's unwavering commitment to diversity and her powerful performances that inspire viewers have solidified her status as a trailblazer in the entertainment business and an iconic figure in the society at large.

Printed in Great Britain
by Amazon

43197429R00040